How to Write a Great Story

A Fiction Writer's Handbook

Othello Bach

Seven Locks Press

SANTA ANA, CALIFORNIA
MINNEAPOLIS, MINNESOTA
WASHINGTON, D.C.

Dedication

To my brother, Don

Seven Locks Press
P.O. Box 25689
Santa Ana, CA 92799
(800) 354-5348

Printed in the United States of America

Library of Congress Cataloging-in-Publication Data

Bach, Othello, 1941–
How to write a great story: a fiction writer's handbook / Othello Bach.
    p. cm.
    ISBN 0-929765-73-7
    1. Fiction—Authorship—Handbooks, manuals, etc. 2. Fiction—
Technique—Handbooks, manuals, etc. I. Title.

        PN3355 .B225 1999   99-046823
        808.3—dc21   CIP

Design: Maritta Tapanainen
Editorial Services: PeopleSpeak

Table of Contents

Introduction

A great story is one that keeps your imagination racing, your eyes glued to the page, and your finger poised to turn the page. When you realize the story is almost over and your enormous pleasure is about to end, you feel a definite sense of loss.

A great story has interesting and believable characters; a strong, exciting plot; natural-sounding dialogue; and plenty of action to keep the story moving. But no one is born a great writer. Just as it takes years of practice to become an outstanding athlete, dancer, or musician, it takes years of practice to become a great writer.

You can learn any craft successfully by trial and error or by instruction. Trial and error, undoubtedly, is the more time-consuming, inefficient, and frustrating method. The frustration frequently becomes so intense that you become discouraged and find that you have neither the time nor the patience to continue. At this point you may abandon your pursuit and never know if you were only moments away from success.

Writers, perhaps more than any other group, attempt to master their craft through the agonizing trial-and-error method. Yet these same creative people know it would be foolish to hope for fame and fortune in any other specialized area without first acquiring specialized instruction and putting in the necessary hours of practice.

Some insist that creativity can't be taught. While this statement is true, many fail to realize that the rules—the do's and don'ts behind a professionally structured piece of writing—*can* be taught and must be learned if writers want to sell their material.

This book covers the basic do's and don'ts of fiction writing. It is filled with examples and suggested exercises to speed the learning process. If becoming a great fiction writer is a part of your fantasy, memorize this book.

CHAPTER ONE

Painting with Words

Learning to write fiction stories begins with learning to write exciting sentences. The kinds of sentences that you write in letters home, answering exam questions, or even writing an article are not generally exciting. They don't need to be. They are generally written for a different purpose: to pass information.

Exciting sentences are written in order to paint word pictures for someone else to enjoy. You select words and mention details that you might never actually speak in daily conversation. You carefully select the perfect words and express your thoughts with the same care that an artist takes in choosing a range of colors and brush strokes to paint a glorious sunrise, a raging river, or a single egg resting in a robin's nest.

A great fiction story is a series of pictures captured in words. It allows readers to meet new characters, visit new places, and experience situations that they would never otherwise encounter.

Perhaps the best part of fiction writing is that you, the writer, are in complete control of the world you create. You control the people, their families and homes, and every experience they have. You are the ruler of a tiny universe, where through your words, others can visit and experience new, exciting situations.

You may write about a beggar or a rich man, and as you are writing the story, you become that person. You think his thoughts and imagine all of his movements and words. The people in your tiny fiction universe must do what you want them to do because you are the ruler— the writer who created them. However, before you can write an exciting story, you must first learn how to write an exciting sentence, then an exciting paragraph. After that, your mind will be racing with new ways to express your thoughts so that you can show others the wonderful worlds you see.

Great Sentence

A great sentence is one that forms a perfect picture in the mind of the reader. It does not have to be long and requires no special vocabulary. It merely communicates an idea so perfectly that the reader can see and feel it.

Most beginning writers have only one way to express their ideas. They use one or two verbs that tell the reader nothing. These two overused verbs are *was* and *were*. While these words are fine if used *occasionally*, if used too often, they destroy an otherwise good sentence and eventually the whole story.

Example

The sun was setting.

There is nothing wrong with that sentence, but there is also nothing new or exciting about it. It tells the reader that it is early evening. However, with a little thought and effort, at least part of the sunset could be described so that the reader can see it. If the sunset is worth mentioning, surely its beauty is worth sharing.

Compare the italicized sentences:

The sun was setting.

or

Long, golden fingers of light stretched across the evening sky and lingered there, as if pointing to tomorrow.

Bill was fat. He was sitting in his chair, watching television.

or

When Bill sat in his recliner, the bulge of his fat stomach almost blocked his view of the television.

Sue was walking across the field, daydreaming, when she fell down.

or

Lost in her daydreams, Sue closed her eyes to enjoy the sunshine on her face. She walked with her face upturned for several steps before she stumbled. Her legs gave way like a marionette whose strings had been cut.

Before you begin to write a sentence, imagine the scene you want to paint with your words. Imagine that you are the character and *feel* what that character feels. Smell what that character smells and hear with that character's ears. For an instant, before you begin to write, see and feel what you want the reader to see and feel.

Use Exciting Verbs

Bright pictures are painted with bright colors. Exciting stories are told with exciting verbs. Dull verbs such as *was* and *were* are weak and lifeless. Verb phrases such as *had been* and *have been* are even duller. The lack of life in these phrases is enough to kill almost any sentence.

Example

It was almost dark. They had been walking for hours when they reached the farm.

Why not paint a picture the reader can really see?

Darkness slowly overtook the valley as they trudged wearily up the road to the farm.

Other dull verbs are
- walk, walked, walking
- talk, talked, talking
- sit, sat, sitting
- stand, stood, standing
- run, ran, running

Everyone walks, talks, sits, and stands. To write *He walked across the yard* tells nothing about your character or his mood. There are many ways of walking, all of them more descriptive than *walk*. You might say he *hurried, strode, trudged, sauntered, ambled, crept, sneaked*, or *jogged* across the yard.

If you can't find the exact verb to suit you, then describe *how* he walked: *He walked with slow and heavy steps* or *He walked with a quick, light energy*. You may also support weak verbs with adverbs: *He walked quickly. He walked slowly and heavily*. However, a strong verb is always better than the best adjective or adverb.

The King of Dullness

The king of all dull, mindless, say-nothing verbs is the word *got*.

Example

> *She got sick. He got up and got medicine for her. She got out of bed. He got her robe. They got the door open and got outside right away. She got sick again. He got tired of her getting sick.*

Got is useless because it only tells you that *something* happened, but it doesn't say *how*. Look at the abundance of information and how the scene is amplified when action verbs replace the word *got*.

> *She fainted. He sprang up and grabbed her medicine. Awaking slowly, she pushed herself up. He draped her robe over her shoulders, then opened the door. They stepped outside. Immediately, she became ill again. He sighed, growing weary of her constant sickness.*

Verbs are action words. Choose verbs that show the action you have in mind for your character.

Exercises

Rewrite the sentences below, using strong action verbs to replace the weak verbs.

> *Julie sat down. Sam stood in the doorway. Later, they got ice cream and left.*
>
> *The sun got hot. It was right overhead. Mike was tired and wanted to sit in the shade of the big oak tree.*
>
> *Tammy walked over to see Tom. They talked for a long time. George was walking over to talk with Tammy when a black cat ran right in front of him.*

CHAPTER TWO

Creating Emotion

Words do more than paint pictures; they also create emotions within readers. Carefully chosen words and well-thought-out sentences can make the reader feel frightened, depressed, happy, angry, or sad.

Even the length of a sentence helps to create a mood within readers. Long sentences with several "ing" words slow down the pace of the story. Short sentences with strong, powerful verbs create a sense of action. Knowing this, you can actually slow the readers' minds and help them to relax and enjoy the sunset that you painted for them. You can also speed up their minds and make them race when you want them to feel excited.

Examples

Longer Sentences

Easing his head slowly onto the pillow, Jim marveled at how wonderful the bed felt beneath his tired, aching body. The pillow, caressing his head like a loving mother, comforted him as he allowed the exhausting tension to flow out of his arms, legs, and back.

Shorter Sentences

Startled, Jim sprang up. The phone rang again. He fumbled for the receiver. It slipped from his hand and clattered to the floor. He grabbed it. "Yes? Yes?" He shook his head and tried to wake up.

If you are careful to select words that paint the exact picture you have in mind and pay attention to the length of your sentences, the reader will love visiting your make-believe world.

Sentence Structure

Sentence *structure* is the way you arrange the words in a sentence. To make a paragraph more interesting, vary your approach to the ideas you are expressing. Instead of beginning each sentence with the subject (noun), open the sentence with a verb, adverb, or adjective phrase.

Examples

The bed was against one wall. The chair was against the other wall. The dresser was against the third wall. The closet took up all of the fourth wall.

As you can see, this makes for some monotonous and boring reading. Even if you continued to use the verb "was" in almost every sentence, the structure still needs to be varied:

> The bed was against one wall. The other wall had only a chair next to it, while a dresser stood against the third wall. Nothing was on the fourth wall except a closet.

While the sentence structure is a bit better, there is still plenty of room for improvement. Take the time to paint a picture so that the reader can really *see* the room. You do this by describing the items in the room and using strong verbs that help the reader see what you want them to see:

> The shabby little room had only a few pieces of furniture. Without a window, the furnishings almost faded into the shadows. A small, unmade bed, its mattress sagging, squatted against the far wall. A tired, old chair and long dresser crouched humbly against the other walls, as if wanting to hide from the shame of their many scars and scratches. The open bottom drawers of the dresser suggested someone had emptied them in a hurry. The small, dark closet held nothing but a single warped hanger.

Exercises

Part 1: Rewrite the sentences below. Describe this room so that readers will feel as if they have seen it with their own eyes.

> There was a table in the room. It had a book on it. There was a sofa, too. The end table had a vase of flowers on it. The flowers were dead.

Part 2: Describe a room in your own house. Give enough details that the readers will feel as if they've seen it.

Part 3: Describe an old woman's room.

C H A P T E R   T H R E E

Learning from Others

One of the quickest ways to become a great writer is to study the writings of great writers. Find a book that you like and open it to one of your favorite paragraphs. Keep the book open so that you can look at that paragraph as you write. Then, using the paragraph as a guide, pattern your own paragraph after it. Rewrite each sentence carefully, changing words to make them fit your scene.

Example

Here's a sample paragraph:

The sun warmed Helen as she skipped down the road to her grandmother's house. Little puffs of dust rose from the ground with every step she took. Her mind raced excitedly as she thought of going into town with her grandmother. Days of shopping with her were always fun.

This is how you might rewrite it:

The rain poured down on John as he hurried along the sidewalk to his aunt's apartment. Puddles splashed beneath his feet with every step. He dreaded days spent with his aunt. They were never any fun.

By using the above paragraph as a pattern for one you might create, your writing will become better. You'll be forced to describe the scene so that others can see it. However, because you will change the characters and everything in the scene, the new scene will be your own.

Exercises

Part 1: Using the following paragraph as a guide, rewrite it. Use the same sentence structure but change the details.

The old lady leaned heavily on her cane as she slowly made her way to the bus bench. She wore a floppy-brimmed hat to shield her from the sun and a pair of sunglasses so big they covered half of her face. She dropped to the bench as though she had taken her last step and never intended to move again.

Part 2: Rewrite a paragraph from one of your favorite books, using the same sentence structure but changing the details.

CHAPTER FOUR

Finding the Formula

Always write about something that interests *you*. What kind of stories do you like to read? Do you like mysteries or romances? Adventure stories or horror tales? Perhaps you like science fiction or westerns. Whatever it is, *that's* the kind of story you should write. Trying to write a story you don't like is a waste of time because no one else will like it either.

Also, any time you're working on a story or novel, limit your reading to the genre of your writing. If you are reading a mystery while trying to write a romance, your writing will suffer. You will always be influenced by what you're reading. Pacing, style, characterization, narrative detail, and dialogue will all be affected. Conversely, reading within the genre of your own writing will enhance your work.

Occasionally, movies, magazines, and even daily life

can negatively influence your ability to sit down and create the scenes that just yesterday flowed from you like warm, liquid sunshine. When this happens, the easiest way to revive your creativity is to pick up a book similar to the one you're writing. Read a page or two or a chapter or two. Once your mind is again tuned to the style and pacing of the language and your mind is alive with similar scenes, you'll be able to return to your work and be productive.

What's Being Published?

Beginning writers look at magazine racks and plow through displays of fiction books excitedly, picking up one publication after another, thinking, "I can do that! I'm sure I can!" And most of them can. However, the unfortunate reality is that most of them never take the time to investigate the genre that interests them and learn how to write for it. It doesn't occur to them that they need to study the genre and understand the essential components before beginning to write.

Just because you have a great idea doesn't mean it's salable. Every fast-food restaurant has its own version of a hamburger, but no two are exactly alike. All fiction stories have common elements, but no two genres are the same. Knowing your genre is like knowing the recipe for the "secret sauce."

For instance, a gothic romance is similar, in places, to a suspense thriller. Westerns and adventure novels have similarities. Science fiction and fantasy have a few common features, but each is unique. The only way for a beginning writer to know exactly what is involved in writing for a particular genre is to *not only* read but discover and learn the formula.

Breaking Down the Formula

One way to learn a formula for a specific genre is to buy a book written about that particular genre. There are many, and you'll probably find one to suit your needs. Most of them are written by writers who have published a number of books in that genre. Some books are extremely informative, while others are about as helpful as reading a bus schedule, so spend a little time in the book store or library browsing for one that meets your needs.

Most publishers of genre fiction have writer's guidelines that they'll send free of charge if you mail your request and include postage and a self-addressed envelope. Others may charge a dollar or two, but it's a wise investment.

However, the best way to discover the formula for a particular genre is to do the research yourself. This requires more time, but in the process you'll learn exactly what you need to know and you'll never forget what you learn.

Develop a table similar to the one below. (I created a table like this when I was twenty-four and sold my first novel to Avon Books.) Add or delete columns to meet your specific needs and purpose.

Publisher	Title	# of M/F Characters	Point of View	Prof. or Blue Collar	# of Compli- cations	% Action, Dialogue, Narration	# of Subplots	Ending— Up/Down	# of Pages
Avon Books	House of Secrets	3 F/2 M	F/sub.	Prof.	5	40/25/55	2	up	168
Zebra Books	Satan's Daughters	4 F/2 M	F/sub.	Prof.	6	40/30/30	3	up	172

Read ten or twelve *recently published* books in the genre that interests you. Read books from at least four different publishers and authors. After you have read each book, slowly page through it again and note the information you need. Fill in the columns and you'll begin to see a pattern developing. Don't jump to conclusions after two books and say, "Okay! I've got it!" Sometimes you'll find enough variation to allow you more freedom than you originally thought. A few publishers actually want something a little different.

By the time you've completed a ten-book table, you'll know *exactly* what's expected of you from these publishers in *that* genre.

A Great American Classic

All new fiction writers dream of writing the "great American classic." I hope you'll actually do it. Unfortunately, there's no formula for a classic, which is generally why everyone wants to write one. (Writers yearn to create in complete freedom.) Equally unfortunate is the idea that formula fiction is not "good" fiction. Before you fall into that trap, remember that the best creations of the most famous artists who ever lived (Beethoven, Bach, and Michelangelo) were all "works for hire"—formulas dictated by their employers. Their talents were used to compose, sculpt, and paint within the parameters set by their employers, primarily representatives of the Church.

The most beautiful bridges and buildings of the world were also created within parameters set by employers. Both time and money constraints dictated that architects and designers call forth "extra" brilliance and creativity. It's one thing to build a beautiful ship to sail on a garden pond and quite another to build it in a glass bottle. Limits frequently draw out genius you never suspected you had.

CHAPTER FIVE

Characterization

The characters in your story are much more than names and bodies. While a character's name and hair color may be important to the plot, generally physical characteristics are not as important as emotional responses. However, when physical appearance *is* important, take the time to describe your character so that your readers will feel as if they are looking at a photograph. Point out details that will create a "word snapshot."

Most new writers think that telling the color of a character's hair, eyes, and shirt or dress is enough to make the reader see the character. It is not.

Examples

> *He had dark hair and wore a yellow shirt. She had on a pink skirt and a blouse to match.*

The color of clothing is only a small part of a character's description, and frequently it is not needed at all. For clothing to matter, it must say something about your character. How does that blue dress fit or that green shirt hang on your character's body? Is the character comfortable or ill at ease? If it's hot, is your character sweating? Are there damp spots on his shirt?

> *The large dark coat swallowed her, making it obvious that it was a hand-me-down.*
> *He tugged nervously at his shirt sleeves, self-conscious that they were too short.*

You may also use various "props" from the environment to help define your characters. The characters' responses to the world around them gives the reader insight into their personalities, just as it does to anyone you see on the street. Let the sun, wind, rain, and objects in their immediate surroundings help reveal your character's thoughts and feelings.

Examples

> *As Sally leaned against the open door, a sudden gust of wind rushed over her. Her long red hair fanned about her face and danced in the lingering breeze. Her green summer dress swirled about her knees, but she didn't seem to notice. "That's nice," she said, lifting her face to air. "I'm glad it's cooling off."*

Tommy squatted in front of the television, looking up only occasionally as he played with the kitten. His tee shirt and cut-offs were almost as dirty as his feet.

In the first example, the wind and the doorway where Sally leaned help describe her. Leaning shows that she is either tired or relaxed. Her response to the wind tells us she has been too warm. Using the wind to fan her hair about her face is a way to describe her hair without saying something dull, such as *Sally had long red hair.*

In the second example, the television is an environmental prop. It helps to show Tommy as an average boy. What he is doing and what he is wearing also tell us that he's an ordinary boy. Using the television and kitten helps the reader see more of Tommy than just his clothes. They show us what Tommy enjoys doing.

Exercises

Describe the following characters. Use props and details of the environment. Write at least four sentences about each character.

- A young child caught in a rainstorm.
- An old man and woman getting off a bus.
- A man coming home from work.
- Someone waking up in a hospital after being in a coma for six years.

Your Character's Emotions

Readers want to know how characters *feel* about what is happening—and they don't want the writer to just tell them. They want the writer to *show* them, to let the characters *act out* their emotions. This means that the writer must show a character's feelings by describing how he walks, talks, and acts.

This may sound difficult, but it's not. You already know everything you need to know to do this. Can you tell when someone is sad, even though he is not crying? Usually, you can. You can tell by the way that person moves, talks, sits, and responds to his surroundings.

Examples

The character in this example is Carla, age eight. She is obviously unhappy, even though her sadness is never mentioned.

> *Carla slumped against the fence like a rag doll. The wind whipped long strands of hair across her face, wiping away her tears. She stared at her feet, afraid to look at the kids playing on the other side of the school yard.*

In three sentences, readers can clearly see a very unhappy little girl. They don't know why she's afraid to look up at the other kids, but she is feeling so terrible about something that readers want to know what has happened.

Here's another emotional scene:

> *The old man's head thrust forward from stooped shoulders, his elbows resting on his knees. His wrinkled, age-spotted hands trembled in spite of his tightly laced fingers. A vacant gaze clouded his eyes as he sat on the steps and stared across the street. Over an hour had passed since the old hound had fallen against his foot, where he still lay. No doubt he was dead. The old man*

knew that. He just couldn't find the will to get up and do what he should do. Such a friend deserved to be mourned, at least for a day.

Show It; Don't *Tell* It

All too frequently beginning writers *tell* about emotions, instead of letting the characters act. The scene about Carla, the unhappy child, could have been told, *Carla was sad. She sat against the fence and cried.* The scene about the old man and the dog could have been told, *The old man was grief-stricken when his dog died.*

In both instances, the writer—not the reader—would have been cheated because such dull, lifeless writing doesn't get published.

However, before you can write convincingly about emotions, you need to seriously consider how people act in different moods and situations. Think about how you would feel in different situations, and consider the numerous ways your body responds to your emotions. For example, how do you act and feel when you're afraid?

- Does your heart pump hard and fast?
- Does your breathing become more rapid? Do you feel out of breath?
- How about your hands? Do they get sweaty or cold and clammy?
- Does your mouth go dry?
- Do you open your eyes very wide or blink rapidly?
- Do you tremble and shake or become rigid?
- Does your voice get shaky and weak or shrill and loud?

It's easy to write about emotions because everyone has them and almost everyone responds the same way.

Example

> *Miss Clark slammed the book down. Hands on her*
> *hips, she glared at the students. "All right!" she snapped,*
> *"I've had just about enough of this nonsense!"*

It's obvious that Miss Clark is angry, even though there is no mention of her anger. Her actions convince us. She could have done more. She could have panted, shouted, or pounded the table. She even might have trembled. We know all of this because angry people act this way.

When you take the time to *show* a character's emotions, the character "comes alive." The reader can see and feel what the character is feeling.

Before writing a scene about an angry person, consider your own physical responses to anger:

- Do your shoulders tense as if you're ready to fight?
- Does your chin thrust forward and do your face and neck become hot and red?
- Do you force yourself to speak calmly but your voice is so tightly controlled it doesn't sound like yours?
- Do you blurt out words you later regret?

Recall some incident that enraged you. Remember how your body responded and make notes for future reference. Also consider other emotions, such as guilt, grief, and happiness. You will use them all at some point.

Exercises

Part 1: List some of the ways your body responds when you are sad, happy, angry, frightened, or guilt-ridden.

Part 2: After you have made these lists, write three or

four sentences showing how the characters below feel
and act in situations that call forth these emotions:

- Sammy, age nine, is sitting in the principal's office.
  He knows he's in big trouble. (Do *not* say he is
  scared or sad. *Show* it.)
- Mrs. Simms, age seventy-two, can't find her cat.
  How does she act? What does she do?
- Mr. Martin, age forty-three, is furious because
  someone has stolen his newspaper. How does he
  act? What does he do and say?
- Julie, age twelve, is overjoyed. She has just learned
  that her divorced parents are getting back together.
  Show how she feels. Describe how she acts.

C H A P T E R   S I X

Creating Memorable Characters

Your character's environment should reflect her personality and reveal any special interests or idiosyncrasies. It should give the reader as much insight into your character as a tour of your home would reveal about you. If you don't take the time to mention details that make the picture come alive, your character will seem to move in a vacuum, and your reader will be left wanting. Great lengths of boring descriptions are not necessary, but a few lines, carefully thought out and stated with genuine feeling, will enhance the scene tremendously.

The way a character decorates her room and home, and even how she keeps the house—whether it's clean or messy—tells the reader what kind of person that character is. While this is not often true of the living room (which is generally reserved for guests), the other rooms of the house frequently telegraph and reinforce the habits and lifestyle of the characters who live there. For instance, what medicines are in the bathroom or on the bedside table? Are there special-interest magazines, evidence of hobbies, or unique pictures on the wall? Are the towels thick and fresh or threadbare and tossed into the corner? Details such as these enhance the character and enchant the reader.

Example

Mary lounged on the couch, her eyes fastened on the daytime drama blaring from the television, a half-knitted sweater on the floor beside her. Two empty beer cans and a half-eaten bag of potato chips littered the table. The chair on the opposite wall seemed to sag beneath the load of dirty clothes piled ready for washing but apparently forgotten. Dishes stacked three and four deep, bearing the remains of several meals, cluttered the small kitchen counter.

From this description, it appears that Mary is a slob. However, she could be an invalid or a lonely, depressed old woman. No mention was made of Mary except that she lounged on the couch.

Readers are much more interested and intrigued when they are *shown* how a character lives rather than being told.

The following paragraph is an example of *telling*:

Mary is a slob. She just lounges on the couch, watching television, and lets everything else go. She leaves dirty dishes in the sink and dirty laundry piled on the living room chair. Beer cans and potato chip bags litter the table.

Create an environment that reflects the true nature of your character. Your readers will love you for it and will remember the details long after you have forgotten them.

Exercise

Describe Mark's room, using the following information:

Mark is fanatically neat. Everything must be in perfect order in his room.

Follow the example given in the description of the dirty room. It doesn't matter if you are describing Mark's bedroom, den, or workshop. The more fanatical you make Mark, the more interesting he will be to your reader.

A Sympathetic Character

Sympathetic characters are good people who have problems, so it's easy to have sympathy for them. Because they are good, we want them to solve their problems. Most stories are about sympathetic characters. When a sympathetic character is also the main character, she is called a *protagonist*.

The person who is causing all the problems in a story is called an *antagonist*. An antagonist is an opponent trying to stop or hinder the success of the main character, or the protagonist.

Show Character Strengths and Weaknesses

One way to show the "goodness" or "badness" of your character is to show your character in a scene with a character who is in a subservient position. A kind person or character will always treat others with kindness. Unkind or cruel people may pretend to be kind when others are around, but when no one is watching they revert to their true nature.

Example

Showing a Kind Character

> *Jimmy crouched down to peek under the bushes. A kitten's wide, frightened eyes stared back at him. "Here, kitty. Come here," he whispered, gently sliding his fingers beneath the bush. "Come here. I'll feed you."*

Of course, you could have told the reader, "Jimmy was a kind boy," but that wouldn't have been nearly as interesting.

Example

Showing an Unkind Character

> *George knelt beside the bush as silently as he could. Through the branches he could see the kitten. It stared at him with wide, frightened eyes. A menacing smile curled the corners of George's mouth. "Get!" he yelled, striking the bush as hard as he could. The terrified animal yowled and dashed to the far side of the yard. The wicked grin stayed on George's face as he squatted slowly and picked up a rock.*

You could have written, "George was mean, even to kittens," but it's not nearly as interesting.

Exercises

Write scenes showing the kindness or unkindness of different characters. Use the situations below:

- A middle-aged woman has dropped a receipt that she needs. Every time she tries to pick it up, the wind whisks it away. (Your character sees this happen.)
- A bird flies into your character's room.
- An employee is late for work, through no fault of her own. (Your character is the employee's boss.)
- A stray dog is digging in your character's garbage can.

Making Your Characters Believable

Believable characters respond to life in the same way that real people respond. Everyone's mood changes from time to time, so your character will have different moods throughout your story. As the story plot progresses, your character will experience many ups and downs. When life is going well, she will feel good and see the whole world as wonderful. When life is not going well, her point of view will darken. Just as you see situations differently when you are upset, so will your characters. Both actions and emotions shift.

Examples

Character: Sam, age fourteen
Situation: Sam is just getting home from school. He's happy because his report card is filled with As and Bs. He's never received such good grades.

> *The front door was stuck again. Sam leaned against it and nudged it open. Inside, he looked around at the*

empty living room. The old couch invited him to sit awhile. The pictures of his grandparents on the mantle smiled down at him as if they were proud of the report card in his pocket. Moving to the window, Sam opened the blinds and let the sun stream in, brightening the room. This is a good house, he thought. I can't wait for Mom and Dad to get home.

Character: Sam, age fourteen

Situation: Sam is just getting home from school. He's depressed and angry about his report card. It's filled with Ds and Fs.

The front door was stuck again. Furious, Sam slammed his body against it. It crashed open. Inside, he stared at the empty living room. The old couch looked dirty and uncomfortable. The pictures of his grandparents on the mantle seemed to mock him. He could practically hear them saying, "You're such a stupid boy, Sam." Moving to the window, Sam closed the blinds even tighter. He wanted to disappear into the darkness of this ugly, old house and never have to face his parents again.

As you can see, the two scenes are exactly alike, except for the character's mood. Sam's perspective makes the room seem different.

Exercises

Write about the situations below. First, describe the room from the character's happy perspective, then describe it from an unhappy perspective.

- It's your character's birthday. He or she has just had a great party. Describe your character's responses to his or her surroundings.
- It's your character's birthday. No one came to the party. Describe your character's responses to the same surroundings.

Unforgettable Characters

Great characters live in the minds of readers for years after the books are closed. This, of course, is the kind of character you hope to create. One of the ways to create memorable characters is to make them physically different. Classic examples of physical difference can be seen in Yoda, Superman, the Hunchback of Notre Dame, and the Ugly Duckling. Another way is to make them mentally or emotionally distinct. Characters who are mentally or emotionally different are unique in their responses. Consequently, we love them or hate them more than other characters.

One of the first classic examples that you likely encountered as a child was the character developed in *The Little Engine That Could*. Children have loved the story since the day it was written because the little engine is physically, mentally, and emotionally *different*. He is smaller than the other engines but is mentally determined to succeed. Against all odds, he refuses to quit, and as a result, he accomplishes what he sets out to do. Readers love a character who is determined and *different*.

Think about your favorite television programs for a minute and you'll see that the characters you like best are always different, either physically or emotionally.

Making the Unbelievable Believable

If you want to create a superhero, such as Superman, you must explain *early* in the story that your character has supernatural powers. Superheroes and supermonsters may be created by mistake or on purpose. *How* they became super isn't as important as telling the reader—in the *first part of the story*—that something happened to give the character supernatural power. Even if your reason is not too believable, readers will accept it if you present it "up front." If you do not explain it early, the readers will think *you* are crazy for expecting them to believe that such a superperson exists.

Example

> *Every time Jan put on the glasses that she found in the alley, she could see into the future of anyone who came into view. Last week, when she first found the glasses and put them on, she saw Todd walking his dog across the street. Then suddenly the scene changed and she saw him falling to the bottom of a well—the well he died in two days later.*
>
> *Now as Jan stared at Mrs. Scott's door, she wondered what she would say. Yesterday she put on the glasses again, just for a moment. She didn't even leave her room. She did, however, glance out the window just as Mrs. Scott stepped onto the porch to get her paper—and the scene changed instantly just as it had with Todd.*
>
> *Her fist poised to knock, Jan hesitated. She had to warn Mrs. Scott. But what could she say that wouldn't sound crazy?*

Different Thoughts and Emotions

A character who thinks differently doesn't have to be explained. The character's words and actions often convince readers that she is not only different but also good or bad.

Another classic character, Heidi, is different because even when she's in situations where others would whine and complain, she accepts those situations and makes the best of them. Consequently, readers like her. They can see that she's different from them, but they know they *could* see situations as she does, if they wanted to. So while Heidi is different, she is not unbelievable.

In *The Christmas Carol* by Charles Dickens, the character Scrooge is definitely different. He is meaner and more heartless than most people. This doesn't have to be explained either because everyone knows what it is to feel mean and heartless.

Going from Bad to Good—Motivation for Change

When a despicable character has a change of heart and decides to become a better, more generous character, you must explain the change of heart—*and the explanation must be believable*. In *The Christmas Carol*, Scrooge has a series of dreams or "visions" in which he sees terrible events that make him afraid. He becomes convinced that he had better change or he's headed for doom.

In real life, people do not change their minds or their ways easily. They must be convinced that they are wrong and that it would benefit them to change. The same is true for your characters. If your main character is a "bad guy" and you want him to have a change of heart and become a "good guy," you must convince him (and the reader) that he has "learned his lesson" and changed his mind.

No "quick" example can be given of this change-of-heart process because the process itself is slow. Realizations about oneself are resisted until they simply can't be denied. Therefore, change-of-heart stories take time and thought. Occasionally, great tragedy prompts change, but all too often it is short-lived. Almost as much patience is required on the writer's part to convince readers that a character has changed as is required to *actually* change.

Exercises

Part 1: Your character has supernatural power and is able to turn himself or herself into many different forms, such as a tree, a thunderstorm, or an ant. First, explain how he or she is able to do this, and show the character using this power for good or evil.

Part 2: Your character is terrified of cats. Show your character in a scene with a cat, then explain why he or she is terrified. This may be told from your character's point of view or by having someone else explain your character's strange behavior.

Part 3: Your character is rude and thoughtless to almost everyone. What might happen to make your character want to be a better person?

Character Motivation

For your story to be successful, your characters must be properly motivated. There must be a logical reason for their otherwise illogical actions. For instance, if a character commits murder, her motivation for doing so must convince the reader that she believed the murder was necessary. The person killed was somehow a threat, and that threat must be convincingly conveyed to the reader.

All the significant characters—the "good guys" as well as the "bad guys"—have reasons for their extraordinary behaviors, and the reader wants to know what they are. If a man jumps off a ten-story building, everyone wonders why. What made him willing to end his life? What situation was so unbearable that death seemed a reasonable alternative? These are questions asked in real life and questions that must be answered when fictional characters have deviant behavior.

If a heroine is too frightened to open a closet door, the reader wants to know why. Left uninformed, the reader will probably decide that your character is stupid or insane and grow impatient with you, the writer.

Character motivation should be established in the plotting and developmental stage of your book. By the time you sit down to actually write your story, you should know your characters as well as you know your family. To "let them develop" as you write is tantamount to saying, "I intend to rewrite this book at least fifteen times," because, undoubtedly, you will.

Consistency

For fictional characters to be believable, they must be consistent. A person who hates mashed potatoes or is afraid of flying or despises rock music in the beginning of a story will hate them in the middle and end of the story *unless* somewhere along the way she has a change of heart. But be careful—changes take time. What we love or hate today, we will love or hate tomorrow unless something drastic happens to change our attitude. If a character changes without proper motivation, she becomes less believable, and the reader will notice.

When developing a character, do not assign loves and hates, likes and dislikes just for the sake of making the character different. Give careful consideration to your character's personality so that his or her responses are reasonable, at least for that character. Once the personality is defined, don't weigh the character down with a lot of unnecessary emotional baggage. Such baggage will slow her down as she moves through the story. If it serves no purpose for the character to hate mashed potatoes, don't mention it. On the other hand, if, as a child, her mother forced her to eat cold mashed potatoes until she almost choked to death and she is now returning to her mother's house with the intent of suffocating her with pounds of mashed potatoes, then obviously it's worth mentioning. But remember, when she stops at Shorty's Diner for the blue plate special, she's not likely to order or eat mashed potatoes.

Quirks

Quirks, or peculiar traits, generally make a character more interesting. Early in a book, such differences often help the reader keep the characters straight. A small gesture, a harmless habit, can go a long way in defining a character.

For example, a man who walks with a distinct limp or a woman who has an annoying habit of jerking her head to toss her hair aside can create a sense of sympathy or impatience. A laugh that's too loud, a nervous tick, or a restless sigh quickly sets a character apart. However, to be effective, be consistent. These characters should behave this way each time they appear.

Dramatic differences create extremely interesting characters but are generally too strange and unsettling to deal with for long. For instance, a man who eats raw meat and sleeps on the floor is dramatically more interesting than a man who eats cooked meat and sleeps in a bed. However, an element of disgust might soon outweigh a reader's interest, and you may defeat your purpose.

Exercises

Develop two character sketches, each at least one page long. They may be from a story in progress or a completely new idea. Give at least one of the characters a peculiar trait and mention it at least twice. Try to blend all that you have learned about developing good characterization to this point. Glance back over the previous pages and jot down points you want to include.

CHAPTER SEVEN

Dialogue

The words that your characters speak are called *dialogue*. Dialogue is always enclosed in quotation marks ("Help!"). When the speaker changes, start a new paragraph.

Dialogue is the one area where fictional characters are quite different from people you know. In real life, people sit for hours talking about nothing important. They bore themselves and each other, and in real life, that's okay. People who love each other are interested in all the details of their friends' and families' lives. They babble on endlessly. However, when you are writing a story, every word of dialogue serves a purpose. If your characters chatter on and on, you will never sell your story.

Bully Conversations and Soap Box Dialogue

For dialogue to be effective, let your characters *share* in conversation. One speaks a few lines and then another says something. As with real-life conversations, a give and take is required. Even if one character is doing most of the talking, the other contributes grunts, nods, gestures, and sounds of approval or disapproval.

Successive lines of dialogue by one character are generally unnatural, boring, and sometimes overwhelming. This could be called *bully dialogue.* You may want to argue that real-life conversations in your house are generally one-sided and that you hardly get to say anything. That may be true, and if it is, you probably don't like it any more than readers. You may or may not correct it in your own house, but you'll have to correct it in your stories if you want them to sell.

Another type of dialogue problem occurs when crusaders masquerade as writers. They have agendas or causes to promote, and they're in a hurry to complete their work. Whether the cause is political, social, or spiritual, the dialogue is always disastrous. A crusader's book is nothing more than a soap box and the characters are merely mouthpieces for "the cause."

Fortunately, the crusader's work is recognizable instantly because of the long blocks of dialogue. The mouthpiece character never has a normal conversation. He may not be particularly religious, but nonetheless, he preaches and preaches and preaches. The listeners (other characters) appear to die of boredom or evaporate into thin air. Once the crusader starts talking, they are never mentioned again.

Blocks of static dialogue are acceptable in only one or two instances: when the character is a teacher or is making a speech as a part of the story. Even then, however, the dialogue should be broken up with gestures, observations, questions, or other logical interruptions.

The best rule of thumb is this: give your characters a line or two, then make them be quiet. Allow other characters to respond with a line or two then gag them, too. Eventually, all that needs saying will be said.

The Purpose of Dialogue

Dialogue has only two purposes: (1) to enhance the character, and (2) to further the plot. Any line of dialogue that doesn't meet one of these two criteria should be eliminated. Never waste time involving your characters in unnecessary conversations. This rule applies at all times, including greetings when people come and go throughout your story. In real life we take time for pleasantries, but these are wasted words in a story.

Examples

> *Tom rang the doorbell.*
> *Fred answered quickly.* "Hi, Tom!"
> "Hi, Fred!"
> "Hey, man, how are you? What have you been up to?"
> "I'm fine, thank you. And you?"
> "Great! Great! Hey, come on in!" *Fred pushed the screen door open.* "What can I do for you?"
> *Tom glanced around and smiled.* "Hey, nice house! How long have you been here, now?"
> "Blah . . . blah . . . blah."

As you can see, this kind of scene could go on for pages, if characters were allowed to chatter to their heart's content.

Instead of writing all the drivel that we actually speak, get to the point quickly:

> *Tom rang the doorbell and Fred answered quickly.*
> *"Hey, Tom! Come in! Come in!"*
> *Once inside, Tom perched nervously on the edge of the sofa. Fred took a chair opposite him. "What can I do for you, Tom?"*
> *Tom sighed. "I came to borrow an ax. I'm going to murder my wife."*

Perhaps this ridiculous example will help you remember that dialogue serves two purposes only: (1) enhance the character or (2) further the plot.

Pay Attention to Speech Patterns

To write great dialogue, pay attention to the way people talk. Everyone speaks a little differently. Even within families, each person has a particular speech pattern. Some talk in long, drawn-out sentences and use a lot of words to say very little. Others speak in short, quick sentences and use only a few words to say a lot. A few are limited to one- and two-syllable words, and others want to impress everyone with their vast vocabulary.

As the writer, you decide how your characters will talk. Decide how voices sound and whether they are soft, loud, high, low, soothing, scratchy, or irritating.

The best way to "test" your dialogue is to read it out loud or record it and listen to the recording. If, when you hear it, it sounds unnatural, then strike it and write another line.

Examples

"Will you come and help me, please? I am drowning."

A drowning person can hardly breathe, much less talk. Therefore, the only *natural* dialogue in this situation would be "Help!"

Now compare the next two sentences:

"Oh, dear. I think you might need to stop the car. I'm going to lose my lunch."

or

"Stop! I'm gonna throw up!"

Some characters will always use correct English. If you have a teacher in your story, he will always talk like a teacher. But if you are writing about children, or people who are not educated and do not always speak correctly, you will give them lines of dialogue that are natural and realistic to them.

Examples

A teacher asking to borrow a pencil might say this:

"John, may I borrow your pencil, please?"

Another student asking to borrow a pencil might sound like this:

"Hey, John! Gotta pencil?"

It takes only a little thought to know how to write natural-sounding dialogue.

Exercises

Write lines of dialogue to fit these situations:

- A mother is running after her two-year-old, who is about to run into the street.
- A woman is late for work and she can't find her car keys.
- A boy is angry because a friend has crashed his bike.
- A policeman is telling a trouble-maker to get out of the park.

Dialogue and Tag Lines

"Tag lines" are the lines that identify which character is speaking.

Example

> *"Get me a piece of rope,"* Jim said.
> *"I can't find any rope,"* said Mary.
> *"But I've got to have a piece of rope!"* Jim insisted.
> *"Then go buy some!"* Mary replied.

Simple tag lines such as "he said" and "she replied" do not tell the reader much about the character, and they become tiresome if used too frequently. Sometimes, however, they are necessary. Great writers have several ways of identifying the speaker. One of the best ways to "tag" dialogue is to describe the action of the speaker either before or after he speaks.

Dialogue and Physical Action

Keep your characters moving as they talk. Hardly anyone speaks without moving. We use our hands. We shuffle our feet. We walk around, pick up items, keep working or watching television. If you keep your characters moving and describe their action and movements, their dialogue seems more natural and keeps your reader interested in what is being said.

In the following example, you'll see how describing the action makes the conversation seem more alive.

Example

"Get me a piece of rope." Jim sat on the suitcase to hold it shut.

Mary ran to the garage but returned empty-handed. "I can't find any rope."

Jim glanced around the room, scowling. "But I've got to have a piece of rope!"

Mary laughed. "Then go buy some."

The scene is more interesting because the characters are moving and acting as they speak. When the characters have longer lines of dialogue, you can also make the scene more interesting by breaking up the dialogue with action lines. You can also add more action.

Example

"Get me a piece of rope." Jim sat on the suitcase to keep it closed. "This thing won't stay shut unless I tie it."

Mary hurried to the garage but returned empty-handed. "I can't find any." She handed him a ball of string. "Will this help?"

Jim scowled at her. "No. It's not strong enough. I have to have rope!"

Mary shrugged. "Then I guess you'll have to buy some." She turned on her heel and left the room.

Contractions

Another way to make your character's dialogue sound
natural is to use contractions. Few people say, "I will do
that." Instead, we say, "I'll do that." We also say, "Let's go,"
instead of "Let us go." Read your dialogue out loud to catch
this mistake. There are dozens of commonly used contractions. Don't be afraid to let your characters use them, too.

Sentence Fragments

We frequently speak an abbreviated language yet have
no difficulty understanding each other. We blurt out
words and sentence fragments as often as we speak in
complete sentences.

Examples

> *"Wanna go to the movies?"*
> *"Which one?"*
> *"Doesn't matter."*
> *"Maybe later. Not now."*

> or

> *"Where have you been?"*
> *"Out."*
> *"Out where?"*
> *"Just out."*

Like contractions, sentence fragments are perfectly
acceptable in fiction dialogue. We all use and understand
them, so it's only natural that your characters use them,
too. Also keep in mind that your scenes will be more alive
if you keep your characters moving, "acting out" the
emotions behind their words.

Example

Two women in the same office are planning a party. They are both angry with a coworker named Marsha and do not intend to invite her to the party.

Betsy hurried down the hall. "Hey, Sharon! Wait up."

Sharon stopped and looked back. "Oh, good! You're just the person I wanted to see."

"What did you decide to do about Marsha?" Betsy whispered.

Sharon shrugged and groaned. "Haven't decided, yet." She moved toward the door. "That's why I wanted to talk to you. How do you think I should handle it?"

Exercises

Write at least four lines of dialogue about the two situations below. Use action lines instead of tag lines to identify the speakers. Before you begin to write, decide what the characters will be doing, what actions they will be involved with.

- Jessica, age twenty-six and recently married, is telling her friend Mia that her new husband is cheating on her.
- Charlie, a shy ten-year-old, is trying to find the courage to ask George to be his friend.

When You Don't Need Tag Lines

Earlier, I said that *most* dialogue scenes are stronger if action lines are added. Sometimes, however, no tag lines or action lines are needed. When a scene is moving quickly and the characters are involved in a conversation, you want the dialogue to move quickly, too. If you add tag lines and action lines to these scenes, you will slow them down and ruin your scenes.

Example

Alan, age six, dropped a quarter and is looking for it. Tim, age ten, walks by, sees the quarter, and picks it up.

> *"That's my quarter."*
> *"I don't think so."*
> *"Yes, it is! I just dropped it!"*
> *"I don't believe you. You just saw it when I picked it up!"*
> *"No! That's not true! I dropped it a few seconds ago! I was looking for it!"*
> *"Ha! Well, it's mine now. Finders keepers."*

In this conversation, tag lines are not needed because it's obvious who is speaking at all times. When tag lines are unnecessary, or when they would only slow down an otherwise fast-action scene, don't use them.

When characters are distinct and cannot be confused, tag lines are unnecessary.

> *"All right, young lady! I told you to stay out of the cookie jar!"*
> *"But I'm hungry!"*
> *"It's almost lunch time! Give me that!"*
> *"No! I want it!"*

Exercises

Part 1: Write dialogue scenes without tag lines. The situations presented below involve characters that are very different. Write dialogue that accurately reflects the speakers, making tag lines unnecessary.

- A police officer and a little girl he found wandering the street.
- A teacher and a first grader who has forgotten to bring lunch.
- Two angry mothers.

Part 2: Write a dialogue scene (of at least six lines) between two people who are approximately the same age and have essentially the same education and social status. Do not use tag lines. Vary their speech patterns, sentence length, and word choices so that the reader can't possibly become confused.

CHAPTER EIGHT

Plotting

E very fiction story needs a plot. The series of problems that a character faces and her attempts to solve
those problems are what make a story interesting.
Without problems and the characters trying to solve
them, you have only a situation. Situations can be interesting but not for long. A great story holds the reader's
interest for hours or even days.

The first point to remember about plotting is this:
every story must open with a problem—not just any
character's problem but the main character's problem. The
only exception to this rule is when the main character is
a detective or a very close family member of the person
with the problem. Otherwise, it is not believable that
someone would struggle with another person's problem.

Plot Formula

The following formula will help you develop your own plots. While the formula is simple, making the plot exciting and believable takes some thought.

1. The story opens with the main character's problem.
2. The main character tries to solve the problem.
3. The problem is not solved but becomes more complicated.
4. The main character tries again to solve the problem.
5. This attempt does not work either. The problem intensifies.
6. The main character tries once more and this time solves the problem.

To adapt this simple formula to a novel, the problem/solution process would be expanded and there would likely be subplots. Subplots will be discussed later.

Read the examples below and see how even the simplest fairy tales follow this formula.

Examples

The Three Little Pigs

1. *Opening problem:* A wolf wants to eat the three little pigs.
2. *Attempted solution:* The pigs close the door.
3. *Problem worsens:* The wolf blows the straw house down.
4. *Attempted solution:* The pigs build a stronger (stick) house.
5. *Problem worsens:* The wolf blows down the stick house.

6. *Attempted solution:* The pigs build a brick house.
7. *Solution (climax):* The wolf comes down the chimney and lands in a boiling pot.

Jack and the Beanstalk

1. *Opening problem:* Jack's family is poor and hungry.
2. *Attempted solution:* He sells the cow for magic beans.
3. *Problem worsens:* Mom is furious and tosses the beans out the window.
4. *Attempted solution:* A tall beanstalk grows overnight. Jack climbs it.
5. *Problem worsens:* Jack finds a giant with a goose that lays golden eggs.
6. *Attempted solution:* Jack steals the goose and runs. The giant almost catches him.
7. *Solution (climax):* Jack cuts the beanstalk and kills the giant.

Tension Builds

A plot should grow more exciting as the story progresses. As the main character struggles to solve the problem, the reader should care more about her. The climax is always just moments prior to the ending.

The following diagram illustrates the movement and essential elements of a plot:

Plot Diagram

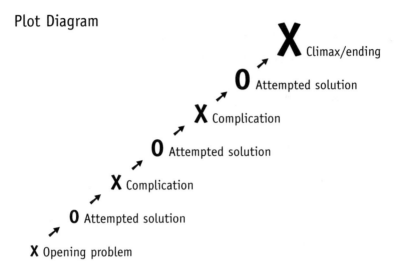

Short story problems can be solved after one or two attempts, but in longer stories and novels, the main character has to try several times before solving the problem. Otherwise, the story won't be believable.

Notice that the plot diagram moves from the bottom to the top of the diagram. That's because the tension and excitement of a story should continue to build until the very last moment.

Who Solves the Problem?

Almost without exception, the main character must solve the problem. If your character is worth reading about, he or she will want to solve his or her own problem. Unless you are writing a fairy tale where magic is happening throughout the story, you also cannot use magic to solve the problem.

No Coincidences, Please

Just as you can't solve a plot problem with magic, you can't solve it with a coincidence. For instance, if David is looking for his long-lost brother and abandons his job and loses his family because of his obsession to locate his brother, it won't be believable if, in the end, he is living in a skid row flophouse and learns—by wonderful coincidence!—that his brother is sleeping on the next cot.

If Sarah is trapped in a cave and the bad guys are coming, you must think of a way for your character to save herself. It is not acceptable to have a bear come out of the woods and eat the bad guys. Even in fairy tales, this is not acceptable.

If you paint your character into a corner, you had better be clever enough to get your character out.

Idiot Plots

"Idiot plots" involve a hero or heroine whose intelligence becomes suspect almost instantly. This occurs when the writer keeps trying to convince the reader that there is a big problem, and the reader can perceive several solutions but the central character can't. A character that continually jumps to ridiculous conclusions is behaving like an idiot.

For instance, a character who hears that a man has been murdered across town and immediately suspects her husband because he left the house without saying where he was going and because he had a "funny" look in his eye appears to have limited intelligence. Then, if without further information to substantiate this ridiculous suspicion, the character waits for her husband to come home, then knocks him in the head with a baseball bat, ties him up, and calls the police, the character isn't just an idiot, she's a lunatic. Any fool can see that such a dim-witted character is creating her own problems, and no reader has time for such stupidity—or an author who can't create a more believable plot problem.

To avoid "idiot plots," make your characters smarter than idiots. The plot cannot be a series of stupid happenings that any average person could solve with a moment's thought.

White Elephant Problems

Another plot problem to avoid is the "white elephant." This occurs when a character struggles for half of the story to gain something, only to realize she does not really want it, so the last half of the story is spent trying to get rid of it.

Example

A young woman struggles for one hundred pages to become a minister. Through painful effort and sacrifice she succeeds, only to realize once she's ordained that this is not the life for her. Now her problem is how to abandon her position without losing face and hurting those who have worked hard to help her achieve her goal.

Keep in mind that if the goal is not worth achieving, it's not a good story problem.

Borrowed Trouble

This plotting error was touched on earlier but needs elaboration. "Borrowed trouble" characters are generally disguised as reporters or former police officers. Apparently these problem addicts can't stand the boredom of their own lives and are willing to risk death for a good headline or recognition back at the precinct. While these characters were acceptable at one time, today's readers are too sophisticated to believe in big-hearted problem solvers. They are not seen as heroes and heroines any more. They bear a closer resemblance to garden-variety fools.

So the rule of thumb on "borrowed trouble" is, simply, don't. The only acceptable circumstance is a husband-wife, parent-child, or other extremely close love relationship. In these, the reader understands that the problem is critically important to the problem solver—or the detective who takes the risk for money. Otherwise, allow the characters in trouble to solve their own problems.

Paper Tigers

A "paper tiger" problem is equally unsalable. This occurs when a problem builds to a frenzied pitch, the reader is salivating in breathless anticipation of a "killer" ending, and the character suddenly wakes up and says, "Oh, it was all a bad dream. Thank God!"

Readers won't be so thankful. This situation is like having a mass murderer chase you all night and when he finally catches you, he says, "Wow, you really thought I was going to hurt you! Oh, geez, I'm sorry. I was only pretending." Once you regain your composure, no doubt you'll want to kill *him*.

If you tell the reader there's a problem, it had better be *real*.

How to Find a Great Story Problem

Problems for story plots are everywhere and in every situation you can imagine. Everyone has problems from time to time, so a good story problem is based on common situations. Problems arise at home, work, or any place in between. They occur between spouses, coworkers, brothers and sisters, neighbors, strangers, and even pets. Sex and money frequently create problems, including murder. Nature also hands out a few—a terrible storm, a freak accident, or an encounter with a wild animal. The type of problem you choose will depend largely upon the type of story you intend to write.

However, not all solutions make good story endings. Most readers like a story with a happy ending. Good people make mistakes; therefore, many stories are about good characters who make bad decisions. Readers identify with this kind of problem and want your character to succeed in overcoming it. Almost without exception, a happy ending will sell more quickly than an unhappy ending.

Suspense Builders

It's possible to intensify any situation by including a time-limit factor. The problem must be resolved within a specific time frame or the consequences will be severe. Be sure to introduce the restriction early; otherwise, it will feel contrived.

A physical limitation also adds tension. When the playing field is not level, everyone roots for the underdog. Likewise, if your character is physically impaired, you will have to be exceedingly clever and plot an ingenious escape or resolution.

An example might be a blind woman who is the only survivor of an automobile crash. Perhaps the car has tumbled down a mountainside on a freezing winter night. She is obviously much more vulnerable than a sighted character. The situation is dire and the tension is greater than if you had used a sighted character.

Avoid Contrived Obstacles

No story is more tedious than one built on contrived obstacles, one coincidence after another. For instance, a woman is about to have a baby. First, the car won't start. When it starts, the woman discovers a snake in the car. Then her frantic husband gets rid of the snake but backs into the mailbox. Lightning and thunder threaten them for the whole drive. A tree falls across the road and they can't pass until the husband moves it. While he's moving it, a mad dog charges out of the woods and attacks him. The woman is hysterical—and who wouldn't be, being stuck in such a stupid story?

If you have plotted a real and believable problem with real and believable characters, you do not need to destroy the earth—one snake, one tree, one dog at a time—to make it exciting.

"What If?"

Learning to plot means learning to think in a clear, logical way. It means creating believable problems and solving them with believable solutions. Once you have decided what kind of story you want to write, a good way to plot your story is to ask yourself some "what if" questions.

Let's say you have decided to write the story *The Three Little Pigs*. Imagine that it hasn't been written yet, and it's entirely your idea.

You might say to yourself,

The opening problem is that three little pigs are being threatened by a wolf who wants to eat them.

Now, what if one of the little pigs decided to save himself by helping the wolf get the other two pigs? What if he helped the wolf blow the house down?

What if . . . what if . . . what if?

As you can see, a story can be plotted any way you want, from beginning to end, by asking yourself, "What if this happened?" or "What if that happened?" or "What if neither of those happened but something else did?"

Exercise

Practice "what-iffing." Develop a new plot based on the opening problem of an existing story.

CHAPTER NINE

Action Scenes

Great stories have great characters who solve problems through great action. When story problems are all mental—that is, all inside the main character's head—the story generally becomes tedious for the writer and the reader. The excitement in a story comes from the action scenes.

Characters *do* things: run, hide, get caught, try to escape, and get caught again. Good characters chase bad characters and bad characters chase good characters. You can sustain interest in a short story with only mental action, dialogue, and narration, but novels need physical action—and lots of it.

When characters are not embroiled in physical action, they are thinking or talking about what they will do next. Where possible, blend mental and physical action. Remember to use strong verbs and short, quick sentences to heighten the sense of action, and your characters will literally act out the scene.

Examples

Showing the Action

> *George gripped the bat. His heart pounded. Sweat trickled down his neck. He had to hit a home run. He had to! If he didn't do it now, they would lose. If he did do it now, with the bases loaded, they would win!*
>
> *Sam wound up to pitch. George gulped. His knees shook. Then Sam threw the ball. A perfect pitch sped toward the plate. George swung hard. The contact jolted his arms and stung his hands. The crowd roared!*
>
> *"Yes!" He shouted. "Yes!" Charging toward first base, he yelped with joy. The ball sailed right out of the ball park.*

Telling the Action

> *Sam was pitching and George was up to bat. When Sam threw a perfect pitch, George hit it and knocked it out of the park.*

Showing the Action

> *Julie knew she would be in trouble if anyone saw her, but she had to do it. She had to know if old Miss Whittiker was really a witch. Slipping around the side of the house, she could hardly breathe. In the darkness, the bushes seemed to grab at her. They scratched her legs and snagged her skirt.*
>
> *"What do you want?" Miss Whittiker's scratchy voice shrieked. "What are you doing here?"*
>
> *Frantically, Julie glanced around. The voice seemed to come from everywhere at once.*

"Get!" the old woman shouted. "Or I'll eat you for breakfast tomorrow!"

Julie shoved herself away from the house and dashed across the yard. She scrambled over the fence and fell to the other side. Crying and shaking, she pushed herself up and stumbled toward home.

The old woman has to be a witch, she thought. No one else would say such a thing!

Telling the Action

Julie didn't want to get into trouble so she hid in the bushes. She had sneaked over to Miss Whittiker's house to see if she was really a witch. It was dark and the bushes scratched her arms and legs. Then old Miss Whittiker yelled, "What are you doing here?" and then she screamed, "Get! Or I'll eat you for breakfast tomorrow!"

This scared Julie so much, she ran across the yard and scrambled over the fence, where she fell down. Crying, she ran home, sure that Miss Whittiker was a witch because no one else would have said such a thing.

Surely, you will agree that *showing* the action creates a stronger image in the reader's mind.

Exercise

Write at least three paragraphs of an action scene. Use strong verbs and short sentences to make the action seem greater. You may write a scene of your own or choose one from the list below:

- Your character tries to save someone from a burning house.
- A robbery has taken place. The robber is being chased.
- You see someone stealing your car.

Point of View, or Who Tells the Story?

The best character to tell your story is the one involved in the most action and who will eventually solve the problem. Where there's action and empathy, there is interest.

The "voice," or point of view (POV), you use depends upon the type of story you write. You have several choices, although the genre of fiction generally dictates which to use.

1. First person, subjective POV (*I, we*)

   Example: *I gave her the book and she immediately handed it back to me. Afraid she would see my fear, I tried to steady my trembling hands.*

This POV is best used in confession stories, romance novels, Gothic romances, and other stories that require a tone of confidentiality. However, because of the extremely personal tone of this POV, it doesn't work as well in other types of stories. The subjective POV restricts information to what can be seen and heard by the main character.

2. Third person, subjective POV (*he/she, they*)

   Example: *He gave her the book and she immediately handed it back to him. Afraid she would see his fear, he tried to steady his trembling hands.*

This POV is effective in mysteries, adventure stories, detective novels, and other popular mass market fiction. The reader feels the suspense of the main character because the single POV doesn't allow for entering the minds of other characters. If your story is being told through George's eyes and thoughts, George cannot know what is being said in the house next door, nor can he know what another character is thinking or feeling. He can, however, draw conclusions based on his observations.

3. Third person, objective POV (*him/her, them*)

Example: *George gave Sue the book and she immediately handed it back to him. He gripped it tightly as if trying to steady his trembling hands.*

This POV is much like a camera. It merely reports the actions from outside the characters' minds. All emotions are inferred or demonstrated through dialogue and action. This POV pays close attention to detail. "Close attention to detail" doesn't mean an overwhelming abundance of details. It means selecting the specific details needed to elicit a specific response from the reader. Ernest Hemmingway was a master of this POV.

4. Third person, multiple POV (*he/she, him/her, they, them*)

Example: *George nervously considered how Sue might respond when he gave her the book. He hoped she wouldn't be too upset. At the first opportunity, he walked up without saying a word and handed it to her. She glanced at it and thrust it back instantly. He wasn't surprised, but still it unsettled him. He clasped it tightly to steady his trembling fingers.*

Sue glared at George, then turned and left the room. How dare he bring that book to her! It didn't prove anything! Jason may not have had it with him when he died. The book established nothing! The click of her heels echoed through the stairwell as she hurried back down to the first floor.

The multiple POV allows you to delve into the individual thoughts and feelings of several characters. However, do not jump from one character's mind to another within the same sentence or paragraph. Clear-cut transitions are necessary so that the reader doesn't become confused. As you can see from the example, this is easily accomplished by leaving a space break of several lines before beginning the next scene.

This POV is popular in novels and lengthy sagas where the motivations of many characters are necessary to tell the whole story. It might well be called the "soap opera" POV because it accomplishes the same purpose. The reader knows everyone's business at all times.

5. Third person, omniscient (all-knowing) POV (*he/she, they*)

   Example: *No one in the hotel knew the two men were fighting on the roof of the building.*

With this POV, the writer is able to see into everyone's mind at once; however, it is effective only for short transitional periods. This POV can't be sustained for the whole story because it automatically destroys suspense and kills interest. It's also impossible for readers to identify with a multitude of characters at once.

After introducing a situation from this all-knowing vantage point, take each character separately and stay with him or her long enough to establish believability and interest without confusing the reader.

Example

No one in the hotel knew the two men were fighting on the roof of the building.

Mable Kerts first learned when she heard a terrifying scream and saw something suddenly fall past her window. Rushing over to see, she . . . blah, blah, blah.

Matthew Simon had just stepped into the bathtub when the phone rang. Annoyed, he toweled off his feet and grumbled as he hurried to answer it.
"Matt?" breathless voice asked. "Did you hear about the fight? A man was just killed. He . . . blah, blah, blah."

Each character is handled separately, allowing the reader to become emotionally involved with each.

Exercises

Using the situation below, write two one-page scenes. Write one from a first person, subjective POV and another from a third person, objective POV.

David, Jessica, and Michael are on a cruise. Jessica and David are married, but Jessica and Michael have been flirting, and David is aware of it. The three are taking a stroll around the deck after dinner.

Story Development

A good story has three parts: a beginning, a middle, and an ending. In simple terms, your story must open with a "hook," an engaging situation that will grab the reader's attention and hold it. Once interest is established, the body of your story must develop logically and steadily toward a climax. Each successive scene becomes more exciting or dramatic than the preceding one.

The final part of your story, the ending, must believably

conclude and resolve the troubles of your main character. If the problems remain unresolved, then you must establish this as the natural, believable end to your story or the reader will feel cheated.

When your story has reached its climax, quickly bring it to a close. Don't drag the ending out with numerous explanations. If it takes more than a couple of paragraphs for a short story or more than a couple of pages for a novel to conclude, then rewrite it. Tie up loose ends early. Readers become impatient with lengthy explanations after the fact.

Exercise

Part 1: Thumb through (or remember) your favorite story. In three short paragraphs, define the opening problem, the body of the story, and the ending.

Part 2: Beginning with one of these opening problems, quickly sketch out a middle and ending to create a new story:

- Jack learns that someone at the office has told an extremely damaging lie about him.
- Cynthia is convinced that the house she has just bought is haunted.
- Roger has discovered a secret place in the wall of his room where he can step through and enter another world.

Turn to the chapter on plotting and use the plot diagram to help you develop your story.

C H A P T E R   T E N

Subplots

S uccessful subplots are natural spin-off problems arising from the original problem. They are usually not as important as the main plot but are often just as interesting. Subplots often develop *because of* the main plot and frequently because of an inept or meddlesome character.

Subplots are not generally used in short stories. A short story sticks to just one plot and two or three characters. Longer stories, however, can have subplots and several interesting characters.

Examples

The main plot of a story might be about a young girl whose family is moving, and she's very upset about the move. She does everything she can to try to prevent it. A subplot might be about her little brother and how he's trying to prevent it, too. Subplots may also develop from conflicting desires between characters or from the main character's own flaws and/or personal problems.

A brilliant scientist receives a huge grant to research a new vaccine. Unknown at this point is the fact that he is an alcoholic. The main story problem deals with how he tries to cover up his mismanagement of both the research and the funds. A complication (subplot) arises out of an auto accident caused by his drinking. Another subplot involves a son who needs him, but because of his drinking problem, he can't help. A third subplot involves jealous partners who resent his receiving all the glory while they do all the work and cover up his mistakes.

Although numerous subplots can be developed from a single problem, limiting them to the two or three most dramatic and emotional situations is generally best. Subplots need to build in urgency parallel to the main story line. When the main problem worsens, the subplots intensify as well.

Using too many subplots makes your story read like a soap opera: no single problem will surface as the central problem. Subplots should be related to the main problem and be resolved simultaneously with, or prior to, the climax of the main plot.

Exercise

Jot down the main plot and subplots of your favorite novel. Once you have identified the subplots, pay attention to how they are introduced into the story. When you clearly see how they relate to the main plot, create subplots for one of the following story problems:

- A young man decides to announce that he's gay on national television, knowing that his unsuspecting parents will be watching.
- A man learns that his wife of six years is an ex-convict.

Your subplots will develop naturally if you simply ask, How will these people be affected by these events? What if *this* happened, or what if *that* happened?

CHAPTER ELEVEN

Prepare to Market

W ho will want your story? If you don't know, then perhaps no one will want it. The easiest way to find out is to browse in bookstores and check out current best-sellers from the library. See who is publishing what. Otherwise, you may write a story that no one wants.

Study the market and become familiar with the publishers. Read what you like to write and write what you like to read. Stay away from unfamiliar lifestyles unless you're prepared to spend a great deal of time researching. Even then, don't begin to write until you feel so comfortable with the lifestyle that you could walk into it and never experience an awkward moment. Poorly researched material will eventually prove embarrassing.

The dwindling fiction market makes it imperative that you study the magazines or genre where you want to publish. Find out exactly what each is publishing. If you don't, you'll waste your time. You'll find numerous books for writers that are extremely helpful. The *Writer's Market*, the *Writer's Guide*, and the *Writer's Handbook* are essential tools for writers. They list publishers, editors, and agents and include brief descriptions of the kinds of materials they handle and what they need. See which book best suits your needs because they are also quite expensive. Work with the latest edition because these books must be current to be of any value. A publisher's needs change almost hourly—and frequently the editors do, too.

Comb the Internet for information. Many publishers and agents have Web sites. Explore all avenues and keep yourself informed.

Training

Training for a writer involves more than just writing. It requires that you learn to think in descriptive phrases or sentences. No one naturally thinks in complete phrases or sentences. Writers, however, must learn to think that way. For instance, rarely do we actually think, "I must remember to bring home a loaf of bread." Instead, our brain sends an instant message to remind us that we need to stop on the way home from work and buy bread. Then, we may verbalize that message: "Oh! Bread. I almost forgot."

One way to practice thinking in complete sentences and descriptive phrases is to pay closer attention to what you see and hear every day. Force yourself to put these impressions into words and complete thoughts.

For instance, when you see a particularly interesting tree all bent from the wind, take advantage of the moment and describe the tree (in thought) as you might in a line of prose: *The old, wind-beaten tree leaned almost to the ground like an old woman too weary to straighten up.*

If a car speeds past you, your brain will make a mental note, but your conscious "writer's mind" must slow down to describe the car and sensation: *The blue sedan whipped around me on the left and screeched off down the road, throwing a cloud of dust back against my windshield.*

Seize every opportunity to practice and develop your ability to describe people and events.

Theme

Every published story has a theme or basic message. Some stories contain more than one theme, but this is generally not a good idea for a beginning writer. If you can condense your story idea into a one- or two-line theme, your chances of writing a salable store are greatly enhanced. By recognizing and identifying the theme, you can direct all narrative, action, and dialogue toward that theme to reinforce it.

Outline

Outlines are the road maps that guide you from one scene to another in a coherent, believable way. Otherwise, you may wander aimlessly and eventually become so frustrated that you quit.

You wouldn't foolishly set out on a trip across unknown terrain without using a map or guide. Similarly, each new story idea is an uncharted sea, and you are likely to drift far off course unless you have a map, or outline. The outline may be as simple or complex as you like, as long as it keeps you headed in the right direction. A short story outline may take no more than half a page (certainly no more than a full page), while an outline of a novel may take several pages.

Use the plotting diagram given earlier to help you plot your story; it will serve you well as an outline. Resist the urge to begin writing your story or novel before you know exactly how one scene follows the next, all the way to the end.

Unlike swimming, writing is not a sink-or-swim situation. You can dog-paddle in circles for years and finally die from sheer frustration.

Flashbacks and Transitions

The flashback—where the writer suddenly takes the reader back in time—can be a handy tool for an experienced writer, but that's generally because the experienced writer has learned to avoid it. An acceptable flashback is an unavoidable one—there is simply no other way to tell the story. The best rule of thumb is to structure a story so that the action stays in the present rather than jumping back and forth from one time period to another.

When an unavoidable flashback situation arises, transition lines are needed to transport the reader smoothly from one time to another. Make the change with as little interruption as possible and as briefly as practicable in order to avoid disturbing the continuity of the story.

Examples

Poor transition

Bill, age forty, is on his way to visit his grandparents.

> *Bill thought about the way his grandmother used to bake cookies and set them out for anyone who wanted*

one. As he thought about this, he remembered his old dog, Pooch, and how he used to slip up from under the table and steal half a dozen cookies before Grandma caught him.

Thinking about Pooch reminded him of when he used to fish in the pond on the south end of the farm . . .

and so on until the transition becomes so labored with short recollections that the reader becomes impatient.

If you have to make a transition, do it quickly. Twenty lines won't convince anyone of the necessity any more than two lines will.

Good Transition

Bill looked forward to relaxing like he had when he was a boy—sitting by the pond on his grandfather's farm, Pooch asleep at his side.

"Bill! Come here!" His grandmother's cheery voice carried through the halls of time and he felt the thrill of it again. "Bill! I baked some cookies!"

Tearing across the field through long rows of corn, dust rising from his bare feet and a strap flying loose from his overalls, he dashed for the house.

"That lad don't like cookies, Martha. Now, do you, boy?" his grandpa teased as he ran a callused hand through Bill's hair.

In this example, it took two lines to actually move the reader from one time period to the next, and then into the middle of the action.

Once your readers have been smoothly transported several times and they know that the story and plot depend on the information divulged in these flashbacks, it is permissible to leave two extra lines of space in your copy to indicate a text break and begin the flashback scene. This technique, however, is best employed after the reader is thoroughly familiar with all of the characters in the past. In other words, don't jump backward ten to fifty years and begin action around characters not yet identified. You'll only confuse the reader.

Also, never interrupt an *action* scene to flash back. The reader will want to strangle you.

Example

> *Richard ran until he thought his heart would burst. He glanced back several times to see how close they were. He ducked between two buildings. The intense darkness reminded him of when he used to slip home in the dark, his twelve-year-old clumsiness always betraying him. Invariably, he would trip over something and . . .*

Interrupting present action for a flashback is unforgivable. Don't do it!

Small transitions, moving your character from one room or one scene to another, can be equally irksome. Handled poorly, they drive the reader to distraction.

Example

Poor Transitions

> *"I don't care if I never see you again!" she yelled as she bolted out of the room. She slammed the door, hurried down the hall, punched the elevator button, and waited. It seemed an eternity before it arrived and when it did, she entered, pushed the button to the garage, and descended.*
>
> *Jabbing the key into the ignition, she pulled out of the stall and headed out of the building. On Fourth Street, she pulled to the curb and parked.*

*She would show him this time. The Lantern Bar—
that's where she'd go. Nothing would irritate him more.
Loud music blared as she opened the door.*

Skip the boring details. They are torture to read and to write. Get on with the action.

Good Transitions

"I don't care if I never see you again!" Helen yelled as she bolted from the room. Determined to hurt him as much as she could, she drove to the Lantern Bar. Nothing would sting worse than for her to go back to the Lantern.

Keep in mind that your readers want action, not monotonous details of walking, opening doors, riding buses, driving cars, and climbing stairs.

Pay Attention to Tenses

The past tense is preferred for fiction. The story is told as though all events have already happened.

Example

He jumped off the horse and ran inside the barn.

The present tense (*He jumps off the horse and runs inside the barn.*) is best left for summaries, outlines, and other forms of writing. Almost all fiction is better told in the past tense. You may be able to find exceptions, but unless you are a seasoned writer with many books published, don't try to be an exception.

New writers frequently switch tenses in the middle of paragraphs or sentences. Take care to be consistent.

Changing tenses jolts the reader and guarantees you'll hinder your chances of being read beyond that sentence.

Example

> *He jumped off the horse and runs inside the barn.*

or

> *He jumped off the horse and ran inside the barn. Suzy screams, "Stop! Don't go in there!"*

Correcting tense variations in your manuscript is a part of the necessary editing you will do before sending your story to a publisher.

Editing

It's difficult to imagine a writer so skilled that editing is unnecessary. Yet many new writers are so in love with their work they can't bring themselves to change a word. Others are just lazy.

If you want to sell your work, prepare yourself to do the hard but essential step of editing. Fill in weak spots, cut wordy scenes, rewrite entire chapters, and throw out characters who aren't carrying their weight. Review each word and phrase to make certain each conveys the precise thought you intended. Scrutinize the details for accuracy, the characters for believability and consistency, and the plot for soundness.

Write your story from beginning to end before editing. This way, you'll be less likely to destroy the continuity. To edit a single chapter or scene before finishing with the story always leads to problems later. Not only is the natural flow interrupted, but more often than not, some plotting detail or character development problem arises halfway through your story. This may mean rewriting your edited chapter, in which case all of your effort will have been wasted.

After your first draft is completed, read it for weaknesses in both characters and plot. When all of the necessary changes have been made, read the entire story again. The second time through, check for weak verbs, lackluster phrases, tense variations, and repetitive sentences or words. In other words, check every word of every line.

Generally, a piece should be edited two, three, or even four times. Never submit anything except your absolute best. Even then, you can be sure than an astute editor will find many ways to improve it.

Example

Let's say you wrote these sentences:

The sun was sinking slowly in the west as Little Feather arrived home. She could hardly wait to see her new baby brother. So she jumped off her horse and ran inside the teepee.

Regarding the first sentence above, you might ask yourself, "Do I want to say the sun was sinking" or "the sun hung just over the horizon?" Do I want to say "in the west" when everyone knows the sun sets in the west?

For the second sentence, you might ask yourself, "Do I want to keep it the way it is or change it to read *Anxious to see her new baby brother, she jumped off her horse and ran inside the teepee?*

Edit every sentence.

Exercise

Edit the following paragraph and rewrite it below. There are several mistakes. Sometimes two sentences need to be combined to make one strong sentence. Weak verbs need to be replaced with stronger action verbs.

Sam saw the old man. He was carry a box. It was tied with string, but he still had a hard time carrying it. The box sort of jumped in his arms as he walked toward the trash dumpster behind the store. He had a hard time hold onto it when he open the lid to the dumpster. Sam watched him drop the box inside. He let the lid fall shut. After he left, Sam went to see what the old man had throw away. But before he got there, he knew. He could hear the poor cat crying from inside the dumpster.

Rewrite your edited paragraph.

C H A P T E R   T W E L V E

Manuscript Preparation

The first page of every manuscript should have your name, address, and telephone number in the upper left-hand corner. The approximate word count goes in the upper right-hand corner. This figure can be approximated by counting the words on a representative page and multiplying by the total number of pages in the story. Round this figure to the nearest hundred.

Skip down to the middle of the page before typing the title. If you're lucky enough to sell your story, this space will be used by the editor to give instructions to the printer. Under the title, type your name, then drop two to four lines and begin your story. Each succeeding page should include your name and the page number. Double space and type on one side of the paper only.

If you sell your story and you have used a word processor or computer, you will likely be asked to provide the editor/publisher with a disk copy. Print and keep a hard copy of your finished work. Often, when your work is accepted but changes need to be made, an editor may call and want to address a specific chapter or page. At that time, it's convenient to have a copy for easy reference.

When you mail your manuscript, always enclose a self-addressed envelope and include sufficient return postage. If you fail to include postage, you'll never see your story again. Publishers can't afford to pay for the postage to return all the material they receive.

Note the date that you mailed the manuscript, then forget that particular story. Begin working on another. If you sit and wait for a response, you'll drive yourself—and everyone else—crazy.

With computers and the Internet, e-mail responses are frequently the fastest and easiest way for an editor to communicate with you. If you have an e-mail address, include it in the upper left corner of your manuscript, along with your street address.

Most magazines take three to six weeks to reply, some as long as ninety days. If within three months you have not heard from the publisher, send a note indicating your concern about the manuscript. Simply state, "I am concerned that perhaps my manuscript entitled *Such and Such* did not reach you, and I would like confirmation that you received it."

If you don't receive a reply within a reasonable period of time, write again and be firmer, but do not be rude or insulting. Occasionally it will seem as if your story has disappeared into some cosmic hole—no one ever responds. This happens with agents as well as publishers. Sometimes postage money is kept and requests for returning the manuscript go unheeded. When this happens, forget it. Make a new copy of your manuscript and send it to another publisher or agent. Most editors and agents aren't so thoughtless.

Sales and Rejections

Rejection slips are as inevitable as death and taxes. Editors receive countless stories every day. Many are rejected immediately because they don't meet the magazines' format or publishers' current needs. Others are just poorly plotted or poorly written. The editor might even have liked your story but just bought one that's similar.

Maybe the editor made an error in judgment. Editors are human, too. How many times have you read about a best-selling book that was rejected ten or fifteen times before a publisher decided to take a "gamble" on it? The point is this: Don't be discouraged if your story is rejected. Keep sending it to those publishers who publish similar stories. If you analyzed the market before you started writing and followed the "do's and don'ts" of fiction writing, you have as much of a chance as the next writer.

If your story is rejected repeatedly, then perhaps it has flaws that need correcting. However, if it's relatively fresh (written within the past six months), you may not have the objectivity needed to catch the errors or weaknesses. Put it away and reread it at a later date. Then you will probably see how the story can be revised and strengthened.

If you think your story won't get a thorough reading by an editor, don't be immature and do something silly like turn pages upside down to see if they come back that way or use a speck of glue on a couple of pages to see if the pages are separated when the manuscript is returned. You not only waste time and energy with such tactics, but you often prejudice the editor against you before he or she even reads your work.

Practice, Practice, Practice

When you have no work in progress, use the exercises listed below to practice in a specific area. Some of the exercises can be done quickly and are perfect for passing time while waiting at the doctor's office or the auto repair shop. Always have a pen and notepad with you so that you can turn "waiting" time into writing time.

Practice Exercises

- Write full-page dialogue scenes with two or three characters.
- Write full-page action scenes with one to three characters.
- Rewrite scenes from published books, keeping the same number of characters and following the sentence structure but *changing the details* so that the scene becomes unrecognizable.
- Write two-page character development pieces, giving physical and emotional details about a single character.
- Following the plot diagram, develop new plots.

Final Thoughts

If you're serious about becoming a writer, then recognize that you've embarked on a difficult but exciting journey—headed for a destination that you may not reach for a while. Eventually, you'll get there. You will sell your first story. At that moment, the feeling of pride, accomplishment, and confidence will be more exhilarating than you ever imagined.

Persist and that day will come.

Othello Bach welcomes you to contact her at
othellobach@prodigy.net